The Law of Libel & Slander

by
Margaret C. Jasper

Oceana's Legal Almanac Series:
Law for the Layperson

1996
Oceana Publications, Inc.
Dobbs Ferry, N.Y.

Information contained in this work has been obtained by Oceana Publications from sources believed to be reliable. However, neither the Publisher nor its authors guarantee the accuracy or completeness of any information published herein, and neither Oceana nor its authors shall be responsible for any errors, omissions or damages arising from the use of this information. This work is published with the understanding that Oceana and its authors are supplying information, but are not attempting to render legal or other professional services. If such services are required, the assistance of an appropriate professional should be sought.

Jasper, Margaret C. The Law of Libel and Slander

ISBN: 0-379-11197-7

Copyright 1996 by Oceana Publications, Inc.

All rights reserved. No part of this publication may be reproduced or transmitted in any form or by any means, electronic or mechanical, including photocopy, recording, xerography, or any information storage and retrieval system, without permission in writing from the publisher.

Manufactured in the United States of America on acid-free paper.

Legal Almanac Series
ISSN: 1075-7376

To My Husband Chris

Your love and support
are my motivation and inspiration

ABOUT THE AUTHOR

MARGARET C. JASPER is an attorney engaged in the general practice of law in South Salem, New York, concentrating in the areas of personal injury and entertainment law. Ms. Jasper holds a Juris Doctor degree from Pace University School of Law, White Plains, New York, is a member of the New York and Connecticut bars, and is certified to practice before the United States District Courts for the Southern and Eastern Districts of New York. She has been appointed to the panel of arbitrators of the American Arbitration Association and the law guardian panel for the Family Court of the State of New York, and is a New York State licensed real estate broker and member of the Westchester County Board of Realtors, operating as Jasper Real Estate, in South Salem, New York.

Ms. Jasper is the author of the following legal almanacs: Juvenile Justice and Children's Law; Marriage and Divorce; Estate Planning; The Law of Contracts; The Law of Dispute Resolution; Law for the Small Business Owner; The Law of Personal Injury; Real Estate Law for the Homeowner and Broker; Everyday Legal Forms; Dictionary of Selected Legal Terms; The Law of Medical Malpractice; The Law of Product Liability; The Law of No-Fault Insurance; and The Law of Immigration.

TABLE OF CONTENTS

INTRODUCTION i

CHAPTER 1: HISTORICAL DEVELOPMENT AND CONSTITUTIONAL CONSIDERATIONS 1

    The English Ecclesiastical Law 1

    The English Common Law 1

    Defamation and the
United States Constitution 2

    The Common Law Strict
Liability Standard 2

    Public Officials 2

    The Landmark Decision of
New York Times v. Sullivan 2

    The Actual Malice Doctrine 4

    Extension of the Actual Malice
Doctrine to Public Figures 5

    Private Individuals 5

    Rosenbloom v. Metromedia 5

    Gertz v. Welch 7

    The Present Law 7

CHAPTER 2: DEFAMATION DEFINED 9

    In General 9

    Libel and Slander Distinguished 9

    Slander 11

    Slander Per Se 11

    Criminal Conduct 12

    Loathsome Disease 12

    Business/Trade/Profession/Office 12

    Sexual Misconduct 13

    Slander Per Quod 13

Libel 13

Libel Per Se and Libel Per Quod 13

Categorization of Radio
and Television Broadcasts 14

CHAPTER 3: THE DEFAMATION
CAUSE OF ACTION 17

In General 17

Elements of a Defamation
Cause of Action 17

A False and Defamatory Statement
Concerning Another 17

Falseness 17

At Common Law 17

Plaintiff Burden - Convincing Clarity 18

Substantial Truth 18

Defamatory Nature 19

In General 19

Context 20

Implication 20

Photographs 21

Questions 21

Headlines 21

Fiction and Humor 22

An Unprivileged Publication
to a Third Party 23

Absolute Privilege 23

Conditional Privilege 23

Republication 23

Repetition 24

Multiple and Single Publications 24

Multiple Publications 24

Single Publications 24

The Reporter's Privilege 25

Fault Amounting to at Least Negligence
on the Part of the Publisher 25

Actionability of the Statement
Irrespective of Harm 26

Liability Without Proof of Special Harm 26

Existence of Special Harm 26

Burden of Proof 26

Plaintiff's Burden 26

Defendant's Burden 27

CHAPTER 4: DEFENSES 29

Truth 29

Privilege 29

Absolute Privilege 30

Judicial Officers 30

Attorneys at Law 31

Parties to and Witnesses
in Judicial Proceedings 31

Jurors 31

Judicial Proceedings 32

Federal Officials 32

Congress 32

Witnesses in
Legislative Proceedings 33

State Officials 33

State Legislators 33

State Agencies
and Administrators 33

Spouse 34

Publication Required by Law 34

Conditional Privilege	34
Protection of Speaker's Own Interests	35
Protection of Recipient and Third Party Interests	36
Protection of Interests in Common	36
Protection of Interests Among Family Members	36
Protection of Public Interests	36
Communications by Inferior Public Officials	37
Abuse of Privilege	37
Common Law Malice	37
Actual Malice	37
Recklessness	38
Negligence	38
Excessive Publication	38
Purpose of Privilege	38
Necessity	39
Publication of a Defamatory Rumor	39
Consent	39
Sovereign Immunity	40
Opinion	40

CHAPTER 5: DAMAGES 43

In General	43
Actual Injury	43
Damage Awards in Private Plaintiff Cases Absent Actual Malice	44
Special Harm	44
Types of Damages	45
Nominal Damages	45
Special Damages	45

General Damages	45
Punitive Damages	46

CHAPTER 6: RETRACTION 47
In General	47
Retraction Statutes	47

CHAPTER 7: THE FUNCTION OF THE JUDGE AND JURY 49
Determination of Meaning and Defamatory Character of Communication	49
Determination of Slander Actionable Per Se	49
Determination of Damages	50
Determination of Publication, Truth and Defendant's Fault	50
Determination of Privileges	50

APPENDICIES

APPENDIX 1 - STATE STATUTES OF LIMITATIONS FOR DEFAMATION CLAIMS	53
APPENDIX 2 - SAMPLE COMPLAINT FOR LIBEL	55
APPENDIX 3 - SAMPLE COMPLAINT FOR SLANDER	59
APPENDIX 4 - FIRST AMENDMENT OF THE U.S. CONSTITUTION	61
APPENDIX 5 - FOURTEENTH AMENDMENT OF THE U.S. CONSTITUTION	63

APPENDIX 6
- SPEECH OR DEBATE CLAUSE OF THE
U.S. CONSTITUTION 65

APPENDIX 7
- APPLICABLE SECTIONS OF THE
RESTATEMENT SECOND OF THE LAW
OF TORTS 67

GLOSSARY 85

BIBLIOGRAPHY 97

INTRODUCTION

This legal almanac explores the area of law known as libel and slander. Libel and slander fall under the general category of defamation. Libel refers to written defamation, and slander is oral defamation. The law of defamation is concerned with the protection of an individual's reputation. Competing against that concern are the First Amendment consititutional rights to freedom of speech and freedom of the press. Nevertheless, those freedoms are not absolute, and carry with them an obligation of responsibility.

Therefore, the judicial system has been called upon to limit these rights, and shape the law in such a way as to promote a fair balance with other important social values, such as the protection of an individual's reputation. If one violates the boundaries of the law, he or she is subject to a defamation suit and may be required to compensate the injured party.

The Supreme Court, through its decisions, has rewritten many aspects of the law of defamation based on the First Amendment prohibitions. Further, as a matter of constitutional law, the Supreme Court decisions are binding on all state courts. This area of law is still undergoing substantial change as there are a number of unsettled areas of defamation law which are yet to be ruled upon by the Supreme Court, as it tries to deal with the competing interests.

This almanac sets forth a general discussion of the history and development of our present-day defamation law, the elements of the cause of action, the defenses, and the applicable damages.

The Appendix provides sample documents, applicable sections of the Restatement Second of the Law of Torts, and other pertinent information and data. The Glossary contains definitions of many of the terms used throughout the almanac.

CHAPTER 1:

HISTORICAL DEVELOPMENT AND CONSTITUTIONAL CONSIDERATIONS

The English Ecclesiastical Law

The law of defamation has its roots in the biblical admonition: "Thou shalt not bear false witness against thy neighbor." As such, it was governed by the English ecclesiastical courts throughout the Middle Ages, until the reign of Henry VIII, when the common law courts began to exercise jurisdiction over defamation cases.

The English Common Law

By the end of the sixteenth century, the common law courts almost completely took over jurisdiction in the area of defamation law. At that time, the only remedy available was an action "on the case" for defamatory words. Thus, slander — i.e. oral defamation — was almost without exception the only type of defamation case heard, although there was no distinction made as to mere form.

Publication of the defamatory communication was essential to bringing the action, and truth was a complete defense. Depending on the existence of certain characteristics and consequences, slander cases fell into certain categories, some of which were actionable per se.

Following the Restoration, the common law courts entertained the doctrine of libel — i.e. written defamation — which was distinguished from slander as being a wrongful act from which damages could be presumed. Thus, a distinction based upon the form of the defamatory communication became law. The reasoning set forth for this distinction was that written defamation contained more malice than if merely spoken. The offense of defamation was deemed a common law misdemeanor in tort.

Defamation and the United States Constitution

The Common Law Strict Liability Standard

Defamation, at common law, was subject to a strict liability standard. Under this strict liability standard, a person who harmed another by publishing a false and defamatory statement about that person was liable if he or she (1) intended the result; (2) recklessly or negligently caused the result; or (3) was without fault — e.g. in the case of a typographical error, or a bona fide belief that a false statement was true — provided harm resulted. This strict liability standard was the law in many jurisdictions of the United States.

However, the United States Supreme Court, in a number of decisions, steered the law of defamation away from the common law, and "constitutionalized" it, as discussed below.

Public Officials

The Landmark Decision of New York Times v. Sullivan

In 1964, U.S. Supreme Court Justice William Brennan handed down a landmark decision concerning libel law in the appeal of *New York Times v. Sullivan*, 376 U.S. 254 (1964).

The *Times* appeal stems from a series of libel suits brought against the newspaper and several Black clergy members, by Southern officials who claimed that they were defamed by an advertisement which was printed in the newspaper.

The advertisement was in the form of a letter requesting monetary assistance to support the civil rights struggle in the South, particularly Alabama. It was signed by a number of well-known citizens. The letter also cited certain racially motivated incidents without naming the offenders.

The Alabama state courts retained jurisdiction over the case, despite the newspaper's efforts to have the case removed to federal court. The first case to be brought to trial involved Montgomery

HISTORICAL & CONSTITUTIONAL CONSIDERATIONS 3

Alabama Public Safety Commissioner L.B. Sullivan, who was awarded a $500,000 judgment against the defendants by an all white jury.

At each appellate level within the state of Alabama, the *Times* lost. Meanwhile, all of the pending libel lawsuits were permitted to go forward despite the defendants' motion that the pending trials be delayed until the appeal was decided. As in the first case, large judgments were rendered for the plaintiffs in all subsequent cases by all white juries.

The *Times* exhausted its appellate remedies at the state level, and requested appellate review by the U.S. Supreme Court, which was granted. In 1964, Associate Justice William Brennan wrote a unanimous decision reversing the Alabama courts.

Although there were numerous technical and procedural grounds which would have permitted reversal, the U.S. Supreme Court instead focused on the substantive issues of the case involving the constitutional guarantees of freedom of speech and of the press.

The decision stated the issues the justices considered:

> "We are required in this case to determine for the first time the extent to which the constitutional protection for speech and press limit a State's power to award damages in a libel action brought by a public official against critics of his official conduct ... The question before us is whether this rule of liability, as applied to an action brought by a public official against critics of his official conduct, abridges the freedom of speech and of the press that is guaranteed by the First and Fourteenth Amendments." [Note: The First Amendment applies to the federal government and the Fourteenth Amendment, Section 1, made those guarantees applicable to the states.]

The applicable text of the First and Fourteenth Amendments to the United States Constitution is set forth in the Appendix.

The decision further stated its support of public debate and the right to freely criticize the conduct of elected officials:

> "... [w]e consider this case against the background of a profound national commitment to the principle that debate on public issues should be uninhibited, robust, and wide open, and that it may well include vehement, caustic, and sometimes unpleasantly sharp attacks on government and public officials."

The U.S. Supreme Court decision rejected the strict liability standard of fault upheld by the Alabama courts. That standard of fault provided that if statements made were in any way false, the jury was to presume injury even if there was no evidence of injury.

The strict liability standard further provided that, in the absence of a retraction, the jury could presume malice in order to award punitive damages, despite a showing of belief in the truth of the statements or good intentions by the defendants. This standard was rejected by the U.S. Supreme Court as having a deterrent effect upon free criticism and public debate.

The Actual Malice Doctrine

In the *Times* case, the Supreme Court set forth the standard of fault for libel cases brought by a public official:

> "The constitutional guarantees require, we think, a federal rule that prohibits a public official from recovering damages for a defamatory falsehood relating to his official conduct unless he proves that the statement was made with *actual malice* —that is, with knowledge that it was false or with reckless disregard of whether it was false or not.

See §580A of the Restatement Second of the Law of Torts set forth in the Appendix.

HISTORICAL & CONSTITUTIONAL CONSIDERATIONS 5

Applying the newly-devised "actual malice" standard of proof, the U.S. Supreme Court found that Commissioner Sullivan had not met this burden of proof, and reversed the judgment of all cases arising from the advertisement.

Extension of the Actual Malice Doctrine to Public Figures

In a series of cases following the *Times* opinion, the U.S. Supreme Court extended the doctrine of actual malice beyond elected public officials, making it applicable to public figures as well, although no precise definition of a public figure has yet been stated. [See, *Rosenblatt v. Baer*, 383 U.S. 75 (1966); *Curtis Publishing Company v. Butts*, 388 U.S. 130 (1967); *Associated Press v. Walker*, 388 U.S. 130 (1967)].

The U.S. Supreme Court has drawn a distinction between a person who has achieved "such pervasive fame or notoriety that he becomes a public figure for all purposes," and a person who "voluntarily injects himself or is drawn into a particular public controversy and thereby becomes a public figure for a limited range of issues."

For example, the scope and nature of the defamatory statement in the latter case may have more limitations, whereas the defamatory statement concerning a "public figure for all purposes" may have much more latitude.

Private Individuals

Rosenbloom v. Metromedia

Some state courts began to apply the actual malice standard to cases involving private individuals where the subject matter was of public interest. The Supreme Court dealt with this issue in *Rosenbloom v. Metromedia*, 403 U.S. 29 (1971).

The *Rosenbloom* case involved the multiple broadcasts by a radio station of information leaked by the police department concerning the arrest of a distributor of "obscene" material during a vice raid. The material was not legally obscene and *Rosenbloom* sued the radio station based on the false reports.

The state trial court set two standards upon which the jury could award punitive damages as a deterrent: (1) if the publication arose from a bad motive or malice towards the plaintiff; or (2) if it was published with reckless indifference to the truth and was in fact untrue. Based on these jury instructions, the jury handed down a $725,000 punitive damage award.

The radio station appealed and the decision was reversed and the verdict set aside by the U.S. Third Circuit Court of Appeals. *Rosenbloom* appealed to the U.S. Supreme Court. The U.S. Supreme Court sustained the court of appeals decision, agreeing that the distinction between public and private persons is unimportant, and the focus should be placed upon the subject matter. The plurality opinion written by Justice Brennan stated, in part:

> "If a matter is a subject of public or general interest it cannot suddenly become less so merely because a private individual did not *voluntarily* choose to become involved."

Again emphasizing it support of public debate, the Court stated:

> "We honor the commitment to robust debate on public issues, which is embodied in the First Amendment, by extending constitutional protection to all discussion and communication involving matters of public or general concern, without regard to whether the persons involved are famous or anonymous."

Thus, for a short period of time, the standard of actual malice requiring knowledge that a statement was false or reckless disregard of whether it was false or not, was made applicable to virtually all defamation cases, except for those arising from the publication of false statements where there is no public interest in the subject matter. In such cases, the negligence standard remained applicable.

HISTORICAL & CONSTITUTIONAL CONSIDERATIONS

Gertz v. Welch

Shortly thereafter, the *Rosenbloom* holding was reconsidered and limited in *Gertz v. Welch*, 418 U.S. 323 (1974). The *Gertz* case involved a private plaintiff, a media defendant, a matter of public concern, and the absence of actual malice. In *Gertz*, the U.S. Supreme Court first rejected the common-law strict liability without fault standard, and specifically held that the First Amendment prohibits *liability without fault* on a "publisher or broadcaster of defamatory falsehood injurious to a private individual."

The U.S. Supreme Court further held that although a finding of fault is now constitutionally required in private individual cases, the standard of mere negligence will satisfy the constitutional requirements. The *Gertz* holding thus repudiated the U.S. Supreme Court's prior holding in *Rosenbloom* which required the actual malice standard of fault in private individual/public matter cases.

Nevertheless, the Supreme Court also held that the states were free to adopt their own higher standard of liability in private individual cases, such as the *actual malice* standard set forth in the *Times* case, if they desired to do so.

The Present Law

Following *Gertz*, the present law concerning defamatory communications concerning a private individual, or a public official/public figure in relation to a strictly private matter unrelated to his or her public capacity, is that the speaker will be liable if he or she (1) knows that the statement is false and defamatory, and (2) either acts in reckless disregard or negligently concerning the communication. See §580B of the Restatement Second of the Law of Torts set forth in the Appendix.

CHAPTER 2:

DEFAMATION DEFINED

In General

The Restatement Second of the Law of Torts defines a defamatory communication as one which "tends so to harm the reputation of another as to lower him in the estimation of the community, or to deter third persons from associating or dealing with him."

See §559 of the Restatement Second of the Law of Torts set forth in the Appendix.

The concept of communication involves the bringing of an idea to the perception or knowledge of another person. It is not necessary that the defamatory communication lower the person in the eyes of *everyone* in the community. A substantial minority will satisfy the statute.

If the defamatory communication is made about a deceased person, the speaker is not liable either to the estate of the deceased, or to his or her family members.

See §560 of the Restatement Second of the Law of Torts set forth in the Appendix.

Nevertheless, the survival statutes of a particular jurisdiction govern whether an action for defamation survives the defamed person's death. Readers are advised to check the statutes of their jurisdictions on this issue.

Libel and Slander Distinguished

There are two components which make up the law of defamation: libel and slander. Libel refers to written or visual defamation, and slander refers to oral or aural defamation. Libel and slander are further distinguished in the Restatement Second of the Law of Torts, as follows:

> (1) Libel consists of the publication of defamatory matter by written or printed words, by its embodiment in physical form or by any other form of communication that has the potentially harmful qualities characteristic of written or printed words.
>
> (2) Slander consists of the publication of defamatory matter by spoken words, transitory gestures or by any form of communication other than those stated in Subsection (1).
>
> (3) The area of dissemination, the deliberate and premeditated character of its publication and the persistence of the defamation are factors to be considered in determining whether a publication is a libel rather than a slander.

See §568 of the Restatement Second of the Law of Torts set forth in the Appendix.

Comment "d" to §568 of the Restatement Second of the Law of Torts further distinguishes the two categories, as follows:

> The publication of defamatory matter by written or printed words constitutes a libel. Common methods of publishing a libel are by newspapers, books, magazines, letters, circulars and petitions ... Defamatory pictures, caricatures, statues and effigies are libels because the defamatory publication is embodied in physical form. There are, however, other methods of publishing a libel. The wide area of dissemination, the fact that a record of the publication is made with some substantial degree of permanence and the deliberation and premeditation of the defamer are important factors for the court to consider in determining whether a particular communication is to be treated as a libel rather than a slander. The publication of defamatory matter may be made by conduct which by reason of its persistence it may be more appropriate to treat as a libel than a slander. On the other hand, the use of a mere transitory gesture com-

monly understood as a substitute for spoken words such as a nod of the head, a wave of the hand or a sign of the fingers is a slander rather than a libel.

Slander

Where the slanderous communication is not actionable per se, as discussed below, it is nonetheless actionable if it is the legal cause of special harm to another. Thus, the plaintiff in a slander case is generally required to prove that he or she suffered special damages, i.e., actual pecuniary injury, as a result of the slanderous communication.

See §575 of the Restatement Second of the Law of Torts set forth in the Appendix.

The plaintiff is entitled to recover damages for the special harm that was caused by the slanderous communication, as well as damages for general loss of reputation, and for any resulting emotional distress, illness or other bodily harm.

Slander Per Se

According to the Restatement Second of the Law of Torts, an exemption to the special damages requirement for slander claims exists if the defamatory statement imputes one of the following conditions or behaviors to the plaintiff: (1) a criminal offense; (2) a loathsome disease; (3) a matter incompatible with the plaintiff's business, trade, profession or office; or (4) serious sexual misconduct, as further discussed below. If it does, it is known as *slander per se* and does not require a showing of special harm.

See §570 of the Restatement Second of the Law of Torts set forth in the Appendix.

Criminal Conduct

A showing of special damages is not required if the slanderous remark imputes to another conduct constituting a criminal offense. The offense, however, must be one which would be punishable by imprisonment in a state or federal institution, or a crime which is regarded by public opinion as involving moral turpitude.

Moral turpitude is generally defined as behavior which is so extreme a departure from ordinary standards of honesty, good morals, justice, or ethics, that it shocks the moral sense of the community.

See §571 of the Restatement Second of the Law of Torts set forth in the Appendix.

Loathsome Disease

A showing of special damages is not required if the slanderous remark imputes to another an existing venereal disease, or other loathsome and communicable disease. To be actionable per se, however, the statement must indicate a present infection with the disease.

See §572 of the Restatement Second of the Law of Torts set forth in the Appendix.

Business/Trade/Profession/Office

A showing of special damages is not required if the slanderous remark imputes to another conduct or other characteristics which would adversely affect that person's fitness for his or her lawful business, trade, profession, or public/private office. This rule is applicable not only to the individual, but also protects corporations and their agents or officers.

See §573 of the Restatement Second of the Law of Torts set forth in the Appendix.

DEFAMATION DEFINED

Sexual Misconduct

A showing of special damages is not required if the slanderous remark imputes to another serious sexual misconduct. This rule does not require criminal conduct, but applies to charges such as unchastity, adultery, and fornication.

See §574 of the Restatement Second of the Law of Torts set forth in the Appendix.

Slander Per Quod

The Restatement Second of the Law of Torts states that:

> One who publishes a slander that, although not actionable per se, is the legal cause of special harm to the person defamed, is subject to liability to him.

Special harm is further defined as "the loss of something having economic or pecuniary value."

See §575 of the Restatement Second of the Law of Torts set forth in the Appendix.

Libel

It is generally easier to maintain a cause of action for libel. This is because libel, being in a written form, is likely to cause a more permanent injury to the plaintiff's reputation; is easily spread to a larger audience; and more readily demonstrates the defendant's intent in making the defamatory statement.

Libel Per Se and Libel Per Quod

The Restatement Second of the Law of Torts provides that a communication which is deemed libelous is also libelous per se, i.e., it does not require any proof of special damages. This was the rule at common law, but only a minority of jurisdictions adhere to this rule today.

See §569 of the Restatement Second of the Law of Torts set forth in the Appendix.

Some jurisdictions will only consider a defamatory statement *libel per se* if the defamatory meaning is readily apparent. If extrinsic facts must be introduced to explain the libelous nature of the defamatory statement, it is deemed *libel per quod* and, to maintain the cause of action, the plaintiff will be required to prove special damages, as in common slander claims. Nevertheless, many jurisdictions further provide that if the statement is one which falls into any of the four *slander per se* categories, proof of special damages is not required.

A *slander per se* which is reduced to writing will usually always be a *libel per se*, however, a *libel per se* will not always be a *slander per se*. This is because a defamatory statement which is libelous on its face, without the introduction of extrinsic facts, may be *libel per se*, but if the defamatory statement does not fall within any of the four enumerated categories, it will not be deemed a *slander per se*.

For example, a newspaper may report that "Mrs. Smith does not properly feed her children because she is cheap." While this statement may be libelous on its face, and thus a *libel per se*, it is not *slander per se* because it does not impute any one of the four enumerated behaviors or conditions constituting *slander per se* as set forth above.

Categorization of Radio and Television Broadcasts

Radio and television broadcasts present a common problem in determining whether the defamation is libel or slander. Some jurisdictions consider defamatory broadcasts to be libel while others have found them to be slander. Generally, if the oral defamatory broadcast will later be published in a written form, it will likely be deemed libel.

The Restatement Second of the Law of Torts states that broadcasting of defamatory matter by means of radio or television is libel whether or not it is read from a manuscript.

Comment "b" of the Restatement Second of the Law of Torts further states: The rule stated in this section is regulated by statute in a number of states; some of these statutes have provided that radio or television broadcasting of defamatory matter constitutes libel; others provide that it constitutes slander.

CHAPTER 3:

THE DEFAMATION CAUSE OF ACTION

In General

Due to the constitutionalization of the torts of libel and slander, as discussed in Chapter 1, the requirements for bringing a defamation cause of action often depend on the facts of the particular case.

For example, if the plaintiff is a public figure, the usual elements may not be enough to form the basis of a "standard" defamation cause of action, and the plaintiff may have to prove "actual malice" according to the constitutional standard set forth in *Times v. Sullivan*.

The standard elements of a defamation cause of action, and the fact patterns which add to the requirements of those elements, are set forth below. Sample Complaints for Libel and Slander are set forth in the Appendix.

Elements of a Defamation Cause of Action

The Restatement Second of the Law of Torts, sets forth the elements necessary to maintain a defamation cause of action. See §558 of the Restatement Second of the Law of Torts set forth in the Appendix. Those elements are discussed below.

A False and Defamatory Statement Concerning Another

Falseness

At Common Law

At common law, the falseness of a defamatory statement was assumed and the burden was on the defendant to prove that the statement was true as his or her defense. This rule still constitutionally applies in cases where the plaintiff is a private figure or the subject matter is of no public interest. The requisite standard is generally proof by a preponderance of the evidence.

However, even in private plaintiff actions, it is unlikely that a truthful defamatory statement would give rise to a judgment for the plaintiff. The U.S. Supreme Court has yet to rule on this issue.

A minority of jurisdictions hold that truth is a bar to recovery for defamation only if the communication is published with good motives for justifiable ends. However, these laws have been routinely struck down as unconstitutional.

Plaintiff Burden - Convincing Clarity

When the plaintiff is a public official, or a public figure, it is the plaintiff who has the burden of proving that the defamatory statement is false. Further, the plaintiff may be required to prove falsity "with convincing clarity," the overriding concern being the constitutional protection of truth telling.

The U.S. Supreme Court has yet to rule on whether the burden of proof shifts to the plaintiff to prove falsity in cases where the plaintiff is a private person, and the subject matter is of public interest.

Substantial Truth

Regardless of who has the burden of proof on the truth or falsity of the statement, if the statement is substantially true, it is generally not actionable, and presents a complete defense to a defamation case. This rule applies provided any false statements or minor inaccuracies do not present significantly greater injury to the plaintiff's reputation than does the full recitation of the facts.

Defamatory Nature

In General

In general, a statement may be defamatory if it injures one's reputation. This is usually accomplished through the use of words, although that is not always the case. The extent to which a statement may be deemed to have injured one's reputation varies among the jurisdictions, and bears on whether the statement will be considered defamatory. Thus, readers are advised to check the law of their own jurisdictions.

For example, a statement which is unflattering, vulgar, embarrassing, or merely hurts one's feelings, may be displeasing to the plaintiff, but is generally not actionable. If such actions were permitted, the courts would likely be inundated with defamation claims.

The key distinction is whether or not the statement will actually injure the plaintiff's reputation. The Restatement Second of the Law of Torts defines a defamatory statement as one that is so injurious to the plaintiff's reputation that it will "lower him in the estimation of the community" or will "deter third persons from associating or dealing with him."

Some form of this standard of defamation has been adopted by most jurisdictions, and generally requires that the defamatory statement have the effect of damaging the plaintiff's reputation in the eyes of at least a substantial minority of reasonable persons in the community.

Of course, the perception of a statement as being defamatory changes depending on certain factors, such as the jurisdiction. A statement which may be deemed defamatory in Mississippi may be held completely unactionable in New York. Further, as the attitudes and social values of different groups change with the times, statements which may have been perceived as defamatory in 1940 may no longer hold such meaning in the year 2000.

Context

In analyzing a defamatory statement, additional rules have been developed to assist in the determination. For example, the allegedly defamatory words must not be taken out of context, but rather must be read in the light of the entire statement taken as a whole.

Words which in isolation appear to be defamatory may actually be innocent when read in their proper context. On the other hand, words which in isolation appear innocent, may take on a more sinister meaning when read in context. The reading of the words in context is also subject to the perception of a "person of ordinary intelligence."

Implication

The actual words will be given their plain and ordinary meaning as the court will not struggle to uncover the defamatory or innocent interpretation of the words. Nevertheless, one may be held liable for what the allegedly defamatory statement *implied* by its words.

For example, *Kerr v. Kerr*, a 1909 case, involved a report which stated that a woman and man who were married, but not to each other, spent a night together in a hotel room. The court held that the statement implied to the average reader that the man and woman engaged in sexual conduct, and was thus libelous by implication.

Nevertheless, many jurisdictions have limited the ability to infer defamation by requiring additional evidence showing that the defendant intended the defamatory implication. Further, where the plaintiff is a public official or public figure, libel by implication must be accompanied by actual malice by the defendant for there to be liability. The constitutional standard of actual malice requires knowledge of the falsity of the statement or reckless disregard for the truth, by the defendant.

Photographs

As previously stated, defamation is not limited to words alone. A photograph may constitute libel if the plaintiff is able to establish the necessary fault requirements. Because the photographic image is rarely false, defamation by photograph also generally occurs through implication. Defamation may occur if the photograph used does not accurately reflect what it purports to represent.

For example, the photograph of an innocent woman promoted in conjunction with a report concerning prostitution may be deemed libelous because it infers that the woman is a prostitute and thus subjects her to ridicule and contempt.

Questions

A similar problem exists when a defamatory statement is made in the form of a question. For example, certain questions may be phrased in such a way as to cast a negative shadow on the reputation of a person. For example: "Is it true, Mr. Politician, that you routinely take bribes from special interest groups?"

Such a statement asked without any factual basis may be deemed defamatory if the sole purpose is to cast doubt on the honesty of Mr. Politician in the eyes of his constituency. However, if there is a factual basis to support the question, and a genuine attempt to obtain information, the statement cannot be defamatory.

Headlines

Another manner in which persons may be misled into believing false and negative information about another occurs through the use of headlines. Many publications attract readers by using seemingly scandalous and defamatory headlines for their articles. However, the article itself may provide the details which explain away the defamatory nature of the headline. Unfortunately, many readers scan the headlines of stories without ever delving into the body of the story to determine the actual facts.

For this reason, some states have followed the old common law rule, by holding that headlines which contain defamatory statements about the plaintiff may be libelous even though the article itself sets forth the factual basis for the statement.

However, the majority of jurisdictions have adopted the general rule of reading a defamatory statement in the context of the whole, in a case-by-case analysis of a particular headline.

Fiction and Humor

Defamation may also be found in the context of works which "fictionalize" characters in a purportedly nonfiction story. For example, an author may not sufficiently disguise the identity of a fictional character who is based on a living person, so that third persons are able to recognize who the fictional character represents. In such a case, an action for libel may be maintained. Again, however, where the plaintiff is a public figure — as is the case in most of these scenarios — the plaintiff must prove actual malice to prevail.

Further, the courts have held that dramatizations may be afforded literary license, do not demand literal truth, and are not evidence of actual malice, even though the nature of the work demands that certain statements contained therein are known to be false.

Similarly, in the context of humor, such as comedy or political satire cartooning, the defendant is usually aware of the falsity of the statement, and actually intends no truth by it. Nevertheless, in such cases, the courts have generally held that this does not constitute actual malice because no reasonable person would understand such statements as having a factual basis. Thus, the courts have generally held such statements to be "nonactionable opinion," and have been reluctant to find defamation.

In defending defamation actions, the defendant is usually required to prove substantial truth in the statements, or the absence of

THE DEFAMATION CAUSE OF ACTION

the required level of fault. However, in the context of defamation actions based on fictionalization or humor, the defendant may also assert that:

(1) the work is not defamatory;

(2) the work is not "of and concerning" the plaintiff; or

(3) like opinion statements, the work is not capable of being proved true or false and thus not actionable.

An Unprivileged Publication to a Third Party

At common law, two types of privileges are recognized permitting defamatory statements. They are the absolute privilege and the conditional, or qualified, privilege.

Absolute Privilege

The absolute privilege affords total immunity from liability to the speaker based on his or her position or status. The doctrine of absolute privilege is more fully discussed in Chapter 4.

Conditional Privilege

A conditional privilege is not concerned with the role of the speaker, but focuses on the *circumstances* under which the defamatory statement is made. The doctrine of conditional privilege is more fully discussed in Chapter 4.

Republication

Republication occurs when a statement is published on a second or subsequent occasion, either by the original speaker, or by another. The common-law rule concerning republication of a defamatory statement is that republishers are responsible for the truth of any allegations they republish, and are equally as liable as the original publisher of the defamatory statement. Further, each republication of the defamatory statement in a new edition is deemed a separate cause of action subject to a new statute of limitations period.

See §578 of the Restatement Second of the Law of Torts set forth in the Appendix.

Repetition

According to the Restatement Second of the Law of Torts, the repetition of a libel or slander by a third person is a legal cause of any special harm resulting from the repetition if that third person was privileged to repeat it; the repetition was authorized or intended by the original defamer, or the repetition was reasonably to be expected.

See §576 of the Restatement Second of the Law of Torts set forth in the Appendix.

If the third person repeating the defamation is privileged to repeat it, he or she is not liable, however, the person who was defamed may sue the person who first published the defamation. The original defamer may also be held liable if he or she authorized or intended the repetition, or if he or she could have reasonably expected it to be repeated.

Multiple and Single Publications

Multiple Publications

Each time the speaker of a defamatory communication repeats the remark to another third person, it would be considered a separate and distinct publication for which a separate cause of action arises, subject to its own statute of limitations.

Single Publications

If the defamatory communication is heard at the same time by two or more third persons, this would be considered a single publication. In addition, one edition of a book or newspaper, or any one radio or television broadcast, exhibition of a motion picture, or similar aggregate communication would be considered a single publication.

In the case of a single publication, the plaintiff may only maintain one cause of action in which damages may be recovered for its publication in all jurisdictions. The judgment also bars further action between the same parties in all jurisdictions. This is known as the "single publication rule."

See §577A of the Restatement Second of the Law of Torts set forth in the Appendix.

The Reporter's Privilege

An exception to the republication doctrine exists for the media who are privileged to quote or paraphrase statements made in court or other public forums. However, the report must be an accurate and complete abridgement of the matter. This is known as the "reporter's privilege."

Fault Amounting to at Least Negligence on the Part of the Publisher

In cases involving private plaintiffs in private matters, the standard of fault depends upon that adopted by the decisions of the courts of the particular jurisdiction. In most jurisdictions, that standard is simple negligence.

In cases involving plaintiffs who are public figures or public officials, the applicable standard of fault was stated in the U.S. Supreme Court decision in *New York Times v. Sullivan* as set forth in Chapter 1. This standard requires proof that the defamatory statement was made with "actual malice" — that is, with knowledge that it was false or with reckless disregard of whether it was false or not.

Actionability of the Statement Irrespective of Special Harm or the Existence of Special Harm Caused by the Publication

The defamatory statement must be actionable with or without the existence of "special harm" as set forth below.

Liability Without Proof of Special Harm

Liability without proof of special harm attaches to slander per se and libel per se, as further discussed in Chapter 2. Again, see §§ 571 through 574 of the Restatement Second of the Law of Torts set forth in the Appendix.

Existence of Special Harm

The showing of special harm is required in cases involving slander per quod and libel per quod, as further discussed in Chapter 2.

Again, see §575 of the Restatement Second of the Law of Torts set forth in the Appendix.

The Burden of Proof

The burden of proof refers to the requirement of the party to persuade the jury to find in his or her favor on an issue, and to introduce sufficient evidence to support and justify that finding.

See § 613 of the Restatement Second of the Law of Torts set forth in the Appendix.

Plaintiff's Burden

In an action for defamation, the plaintiff has the burden of proving the following issues when they are properly raised in the case:

1. The defamatory character of the communication;

2. Publication of the communication by the defendant;

3. Application of the communication to the plaintiff;

THE DEFAMATION CAUSE OF ACTION

4. The recipient's understanding of the defamatory meaning of the statement;

5. The recipient's understanding that the statement was intended to apply to the plaintiff;

6. Special harm resulting to the plaintiff from publication of the statement;

7. The defendant's negligence, reckless disregard or knowledge regarding the truth or falsity and defamatory character of the communication; and

8. The defendant's abuse of a conditional privilege.

Defendant's Burden

In an action for defamation, the defendant has the burden of proving, when the issue is properly raised, the presence of the circumstances necessary for the existence of a privilege to publish the defamatory communication.

Further, in certain cases involving private individuals, the defendant may still retain the burden of proving the truth of the defamatory statement. In cases which involve public officials/public figures, this burden has been shifted to the plaintiff to prove the defendant's negligence or greater fault regarding the falsity of the statement. However, this issue is not yet settled by the U.S. Supreme Court in cases involving private plaintiffs.

CHAPTER 4:

DEFENSES

The primary defenses to a claim for defamation are set forth below.

Truth

At common law, truth was considered an absolute defense to a claim of defamation. Truth is still generally available as a defense in cases involving private plaintiffs concerning matters of no public interest.

See §581A of the Restatement Second of the Law of Torts set forth in the Appendix.

Although the doctrine that truth is generally inactionable still holds true, constitutional considerations in cases involving public plaintiffs, or issues of public concern, have shifted the burden of proof to the plaintiff, who must demonstrate the falsity of the statement. The plaintiff's burden of proof is more fully discussed in Chapter 3.

Further, some jurisdictions have enacted constitutional or statutory provisions which bar truth as a defense if the statement is: (1) published for malicious motives; (2) if there is no justifiable purpose for publishing the statement; or (3) if the statement concerns matters of public interest.

Privilege

At common law, there are two types of privileges which enable an individual to make defamatory statements. They are (1) absolute privilege; and (2) conditional privilege — also known as "qualified privilege."

Absolute Privilege

The existence of absolute privilege depends on the speaker's position or status. If the speaker is entitled to absolute privilege, he or she is given total immunity from liability for defamatory statements. Absolute privilege extends to certain public officials in the course of performing their official duties, as set forth below.

The rationale for granting this absolute privilege is the notion that individuals in certain positions require complete freedom of speech so that their duties may be properly carried out.

If an individual is deemed to be entitled to absolute privilege, personal motives cannot thereafter be imputed if the defamatory statement is made while the individual is acting in his or her official capacity. Therefore, evidence of recklessness or malice is irrelevant and will not defeat the immunity.

Positions for which absolute privilege applies include:

Judicial Officers

Absolute privilege is granted to any person who acts as a judge, and who presides over courts of both limited and general jurisdiction. It also applies to others who perform judicial functions, such as members of military tribunals. However, the immunity only applies to communications which are within the scope of the judge's duties.

The personal malice of the judge, or the fact that he or she knew the defamatory communication to be false, would be irrelevant. Thus, the judge could not be subjected to an action for defamation if the judge is acting within the scope of his or her official duties. Nevertheless, a judge who abuses his or her official position may be impeached or removed.

See §585 of the Restatement Second of the Law of Torts set forth in the Appendix.

Attorneys At Law

Absolute privilege is granted to lawyers in connection with the institution of lawsuits, and during the course of judicial proceedings, in which they participate as counsel. The immunity applies to all aspects of the lawyer's representation, such as settlement discussions, litigation documents, discovery proceedings, and trial procedure.

Nevertheless, the privileged statements must have some bearing on the proposed or pending judicial proceeding. If defamatory communications are made when there is no intention to institute a lawsuit, or the communication is unrelated to any contemplated or pending litigation, those defamatory comments would not be protected.

See §586 of the Restatement Second of the Law of Torts set forth in the Appendix.

Parties To and Witness in Judicial Proceedings

Parties to, and witnesses in, a judicial proceeding are entitled to the same absolute privilege as lawyers provided that the defamatory communication is related to the judicial proceeding. The rationale is that the search for the truth should not be restrained by the witnesses' concern that they may be sued for statements they make in relation to the controversy.

Further, this immunity is so absolute that even testimony which is proved to be perjurious cannot be the basis for a defamation lawsuit against the witness.

See §§ 586 and 587 of the Restatement Second of the Law of Torts set forth in the Appendix.

Jurors

Jury members of a grand or petit jury are given absolute privilege for defamatory statements made during the course of their service on the jury. This would include defamatory statements made against a fellow juror, the judge, the parties, witnesses, and lawyers, again provided that the defamatory comments are related to the judicial proceeding.

See §589 of the Restatement Second of the Law of Torts set forth in the Appendix.

Judicial Proceedings

As set forth above, all participants in a judicial proceeding are afforded immunity in connection with defamatory statements made in relation to the proceeding, whether made in or out of the courtroom. However, the privilege does not extend to out-of-court defamatory statements made to members of the media, or third parties not involved in the litigation, and the speakers may be held liable for such comments.

In order to defeat this immunity, the defamatory statement must be clearly and completely unrelated to the judicial proceeding. If there is any doubt that the statement is pertinent, it will be deemed privileged.

Federal Officials

Federal officials are also immune from liability for defamatory statements made during the course of their official duties. However, if the defamatory comment is not within the scope of duty, the immunity will not attach.

See § 591 of the Restatement Second of the Law of Torts set forth in the Appendix.

Congress

Pursuant to Article I, Section 6 of the U.S. Constitution ("The Speech or Debate Clause"), members of Congress are immune from liability for defamatory statements made during the course of their speeches or debates. This immunity is not confined to statements made while on the floor of either House, however, the Supreme Court has held that the Speech or Debate Clause protects only those statements made in the course of legislative activities.

The applicable text of the Speech of Debate Clause of the U.S. Constitution is set forth in the Appendix.

Also, see §590 of the Restatement Second of the Law of Torts set forth in the Appendix.

> Witnesses in legislative proceedings are absolutely privileged to publish defamatory statements as part of the legislative proceeding in which the witness is testifying, or in communications preliminary to the proceeding, provided that the statement is related to the proceeding.

See §590A of the Restatement Second of the Law of Torts set forth in the Appendix.

State Officials

State Legislators

Although the Speech or Debate Clause of the U.S. Constitution refers to members of the United States Congress, similar provisions are contained in most state constitutions which provide substantially the same immunity to state legislative officials.

Again, see §590 of the Restatement Second of the Law of Torts set forth in the Appendix.

State Agencies and Administrators

Absolute immunity for defamatory statements has been held to apply to statements made before state agencies and administrative bodies, again provided that the defamatory statement is related to the proceeding and the speaker is acting within his or her official capacity. This privilege also applies to state executive officers at the highest levels, and certain state officials.

Again, see §591 of the Restatement Second of the Law of Torts set forth in the Appendix.

The privilege afforded members of subordinate state legislative bodies, and lower-level state executives and officials, may not be absolute dependent upon the particular state's law. The reader is cautioned to check the law of their own jurisdictions.

Spouse

A husband or wife has an absolute privilege to make defamatory statements to each other concerning a third person. This privilege is based on the confidential nature of the spousal relationship. Originally, the rationale for this privilege was that the marital couple is one being, thus no publication of the defamatory statement to a third person is made.

See §592 of the Restatement Second of the Law of Torts set forth in the Appendix.

Publication Required by Law

Absolute privilege attaches to any publication which is required by law. For example, if a newspaper is required by law to publish a legal notice, it is immune from liability resulting for any alleged defamatory matter contained in the notice.

See §592A of the Restatement Second of the Law of Torts set forth in the Appendix.

Conditional Privilege

Conditional privilege is not concerned with the role of the speaker, but focuses on the *circumstances* under which the defamatory statement was made.

At common law, the defendant was permitted to plead and prove that he or she had either a duty to make the defamatory statement, or a legitimate interest to protect by making it. To obtain this privilege, however, the "speaker" must act in good faith, without malice, and without abusing the privilege.

The rationale underlying this privilege is that, under certain circumstances, the good that may be accomplished by permitting someone to make a defamatory statement without fear of liability outweighs the harm that may be done to the reputation of others.

An example of conditional privilege is the generally recognized right of credit reporting agencies to gather information concerning an individual, and provide this information to a subscriber for the purpose of extending credit to the individual.

These credit reports may contain negative information, which may be false or outdated, concerning the credit profile of the individual. However, absent a showing of recklessness, bad faith, or malicious intent, the privilege will likely be upheld.

The Restatement Second of the Law of Torts has set forth six circumstances in which a person has a conditional or qualified privilege to make defamatory statements, as discussed below:

Protection of the Speaker's Own Interests

Defamatory statements made by the speaker to protect his or her own interests are conditionally privileged. However, that interest must be sufficiently important, and the recipient of the defamatory communication must be a proper person charged with protection of that interest.

For example, a crime victim is immune from liability for defamatory statements made to the police concerning the alleged perpetrator.

See §594 of the Restatement Second of the Law of Torts set forth in the Appendix.

Protection of Recipient or Third Party Interests

Defamatory statements made by the speaker to protect sufficiently important interests of the recipient or a third party are conditionally privileged. However, the speaker must be under some type of duty, such as a legal duty, to make the statement.

See §595 of the Restatement Second of the Law of Torts set forth in the Appendix.

Protection of Interests in Common

Defamatory statements made by the speaker to protect a sufficiently important common interest by the speaker and the recipient are conditionally privileged. This usually occurs in situations where one or more persons having a common interest in a particular matter believe that information exists concerning that common interest which another is entitled to know. A common example would be the privilege afforded members of a tenants' rights organization.

See §596 of the Restatement Second of the Law of Torts set forth in the Appendix.

Protection of Interests Among Family Members

Defamatory statements made among members of a family, or between one family member and a third party concerning another family member, are conditionally privileged.

See §597 of the Restatement Second of the Law of Torts set forth in the Appendix.

Protection of Public Interests

Defamatory statements made to a third party who has the authority to act in the public interest are conditionally privileged. For example, a complaint by a citizen to the supervisor of a city bus driver who was allegedly driving in a reckless manner would be protected.

See §598 of the Restatement Second of the Law of Torts set forth in the Appendix.

Communications by Inferior Public Officials

Defamatory statements made by public officials in the course of their official duties who are not entitled to absolute privilege are conditionally privileged.

See §598A of the Restatement Second of the Law of Torts set forth in the Appendix.

Abuse of Privilege

There are certain circumstances which will defeat the privilege to make defamatory statements with immunity, as set forth below.

Common-Law Malice

A showing of malice towards the plaintiff will defeat a claim of conditional privilege if the plaintiff can show that the defamatory statement was unrelated to the privilege claimed, and that there existed a predominant improper motivation on the part of the speaker, including spite, ill will, hatred or the intention to inflict harm.

Actual Malice

Actual malice is the constitutional standard of malice concerned with the defendant's disregard for truth, rather than his or her ill will towards the plaintiff. Actual malice has been defined as publication of a defamatory statement with knowledge of its falsity or subjective awareness of its probable falsity. Actual malice has been deemed evidence of common-law malice in order to defeat conditional privilege because the Courts have reasoned that there is no valid reason to protect the interests of a liar.

See §600 of the Restatement Second of the Law of Torts set forth in the Appendix.

Recklessness

Recklessly false statements have been held to be conclusive evidence of common-law malice for the purpose of defeating conditional privilege because it demonstrates ill will on the part of the speaker.

Negligence

Negligence is defined as a lack of reasonable grounds for belief in the truth of a defamatory statement. Courts are divided as to whether negligence on the part of the speaker should defeat the conditional privilege.

Excessive Publication

Excessive publication of a defamatory statement to a person who is not the proper recipient of such communication abuses the privilege.

See §604 of the Restatement Second of the Law of Torts set forth in the Appendix.

Purpose of Privilege

If one who is entitled to a conditional privilege publishes defamatory statements concerning another absent any purpose for protecting the interest for which the privilege is given, he or she abuses the privilege.

See §603 of the Restatement Second of the Law of Torts set forth in the Appendix.

Necessity

If one who is entitled to a conditional privilege publishes defamatory statements concerning another without a reasonable belief that the statement is necessary to accomplish the purpose for which the privilege was given, he or she abuses the privilege.

See §605 of the Restatement Second of the Law of Torts set forth in the Appendix.

Publication of a Defamatory Rumor

If one who is entitled to a conditional privilege publishes a defamatory rumor or suspicion, he or she does not abuse the privilege, even if he or she knows or believes the rumor or suspicion to be false, provided that (1) the defamatory matter is stated as rumor or suspicion and not fact, and (2) the publication is reasonable based upon the relationship of the parties, the importance of the interests affected, and the harm likely to result.

See §602 of the Restatement Second of the Law of Torts set forth in the Appendix.

Consent

Consent to the publication of a defamatory statement by the person who has been defamed, is a complete defense to any cause of action for defamation by that person. However, the nature of the consent must be examined to determine the scope of the consent given.

This rule applies even if the person does not know that the statements to which he or she is consenting are, or will be, defamatory. It is sufficient if he or she is aware of the exact language of the publication, or that it may be defamatory.

For example, an employee who was fired from a previous job due to habitual lateness and absence requests that his former employer send a statement indicating the reasons the employee was fired to a potential employer. Employer #1 sends a letter indicating the reason. Employee is not hired by Employer #2. Employer #1 would not be liable for defamation. Employee took the risk that the statement would be defamatory and consented to its publication.

It has been held that conduct which gives apparent consent sufficiently bars recovery. Further, if the person to whom the consent is given reasonably interprets the conduct as consent to the publication of the defamatory matter for all purposes, the publication would be likely be privileged. However, if the consent is limited to publication to a particular individual, or for a particular purpose or time, those limitations must be adhered to for the privilege to attach.

See §583 of the Restatement Second of the Law of Torts set forth in the Appendix.

Sovereign Immunity

The federal government has absolute sovereign immunity against all tort claims, unless specifically waived by statute. The federal government has not waived its immunity from defamation claims. State governments also have sovereign immunity from tort claims unless specifically waived by statute. The reader is cautioned to check the law of their own jurisdictions when contemplating a defamation claim against a particular state.

Opinion

At common law, the privilege of "fair comment" was a defense to a defamation claim. This doctrine was inspired by the same concern for freedom of expression and free debate which motivated the constitutionalization of defamation law by the U.S. Supreme Court.

The "fair comment" doctrine was deemed inadequate due to the uncertainty of its application, which could deter the freedom of expression it purported to protect. A speaker was still subject to a

DEFENSES

judge or jury's interpretation of whether his or her comments were fair or unfair, opinion or fact.

The U.S. Supreme Court sought to correct this uncertainty through a series of cases beginning with its 1974 decision in *Gertz v. Robert Welch*. In *Gertz*, the court rejected the notion that the correctness of an opinion be ruled upon by a judge or jury, and further stated that: "Under the First Amendment, there is no such thing as a false idea." Following *Gertz*, the majority of courts have ruled that opinion is constitutionally protected speech and not actionable.

CHAPTER 5:

DAMAGES

In General

Damages sustained on account of libel or slander are particularly difficult to calculate because measurable pecuniary losses are usually not significant in defamation cases.

Actual Injury

The U.S. Supreme Court, in its holding in the *Gertz* case, recognized that "actual injury" as a result of being defamed is not limited to out-of-pocket expenses, but may include such items as:

(1) impairment of reputation and standing in the community;

(2) personal humiliation; and

(3) mental anguish and suffering, and any resulting bodily harm.

See §623 of the Restatement Second of the Law of Torts set forth in the Appendix.

The *Gertz* case involved a private plaintiff and a media defendant. The amount of the damage award in such cases is within the discretion of the jury, and often results in very large plaintiff verdicts, particularly in libel cases such as *Gertz* which involve media defendants.

For this reason, the U.S. Supreme Court refused to allow punitive damage awards in private plaintiff cases against media defendants, reasoning that "jury discretion to award punitive damages unnecessarily exacerbates the danger of media self-censorship."

Damage Awards in Private Plaintiff Cases Absent Actual Malice

In *Gertz*, the Supreme Court further set forth certain criteria which should be considered by the jury in private plaintiff cases where actual malice was not established, as follows:

(1) damages must be supported by competent evidence;

(2) compensation must not exceed actual injury;

(3) damages may not be presumed; and

(4) damages must not constitute punitive damages in disguise.

This criteria appears to exclude cases where the standard of *actual malice* is proven, as set forth in *New York Times v. Sullivan*. The U.S. Supreme Court later held that the *Gertz* rules do not necessarily apply to cases involving a private plaintiff where the defamatory statements are not matters of public interest.

Special Harm

The Restatement Second of the Law of Torts provides that one who is liable for either a slander actionable per se or a libel is also liable for any special harm legally caused by the defamatory publication.

The Restatement further states that defamation is a legal cause of special harm to the person defamed if it is both (1) a substantial factor in bringing about the harm, and (2) there is no rule of law relieving the publisher from liability because of the manner in which the publication has resulted in the harm.

See §§622 and 622A of the Restatement Second of the Law of Torts set forth in the Appendix.

DAMAGES

Types of Damages

Nominal Damages

The Restatement Second of the Law of Torts provides that one who is liable for a slander actionable per se or a libel is liable for at least nominal damages.

Nominal damages are awards of insignificant sums of money, e.g. one dollar, in order to vindicate the plaintiff's reputation rather than to compensate the plaintiff for any losses sustained. A nominal damage award may result if the jury does not believe that substantial harm has resulted from the defamation.

Nevertheless, in cases where punitive damages are available, an insignificant nominal damage award may support a large punitive damage award.

See §620 of the Restatement Second of the Law of Torts set forth in the Appendix.

Special Damages

Special damages refers to compensation awarded the plaintiff for actual pecuniary loss capable of calculation. Special damages must be pleaded and proved with particularity. It is difficult to prove special damages in libel and slander suits. The plaintiff must demonstrate that the pecuniary loss was directly related to the injury to reputation caused by the defamation.

General Damages

General damages refers to compensation awarded the plaintiff for presumed and actual injury. At common law, where the defamatory statements were actionable *per se*, damages were presumed and the plaintiff was entitled, as a matter of law, to compensatory damages without proving special damages. Juries may award significant "presumed damages" with very little instruction by the court.

See §621 of the Restatement Second of the Law of Torts set forth in the Appendix.

The *Gertz* case eliminated presumed damages as unconstitutional in private plaintiff/media defendant cases involving matters of public interest where actual malice is not proven. However, the Court permitted recovery for actual injury, according to the criteria set forth above.

Punitive Damages

Punitive damages, also known as exemplary damages, refers to compensation awarded the plaintiff in order to punish the defendant and deter future like behavior by the same defendant or others.

The Supreme Court has subjected punitive damage awards to a "reasonableness" test. However, as set forth in *Gertz*, the Court is concerned with the effect that a large punitive damage award could have on the constitutional rights of freedom of expression. Therefore, they have denied punitive damages awards in private plaintiff/media defendant cases involving matters of public interest, where there is no proof of actual malice.

In addition, in cases where actual malice is proven, the standard of proof requires clear and convincing evidence in order for a punitive damage award to apply. Some courts have further held that actual malice is not enough to support a punitive damage award, but further evidence of common-law malice is required.

CHAPTER 6:

RETRACTION

In General

At common law, a defendant could offer to retract the defamatory statement in order to mitigate damages, and to negate common-law or actual malice. This would be to the defendant's advantage because, without proof of malice, a punitive damage award may be unavailable to the plaintiff. Further, a prompt retraction may serve to reduce the compensatory damages to which the plaintiff may be entitled.

Retraction Statutes

The majority of jurisdictions have enacted legislation governing the retraction procedure. Most retraction statutes only apply to cases involving media defendants concerning statements made in good faith, e.g. by mistake.

Although the statutes differ according to the jurisdiction, they generally require the plaintiff to serve written notice upon the publisher, demanding retraction of the defamatory statement, within a specified time limit. This requirement may be a condition precedent to bringing the defamation lawsuit.

If a proper retraction is then published in a timely manner, the damage award to the plaintiff may be limited. A proper retraction would generally be one which is full and unequivocal, and made in at least the same medium and manner as the original defamatory statement. Some statutes require additional specifications, such as front page publication of the retraction, or use of a specific type size.

Readers are advised to check the law of their own jurisdictions concerning the provisions of its retraction statute, if any.

CHAPTER 7:

THE FUNCTION OF THE JUDGE AND JURY

This chapter discusses the function of the judge and jury in deciding the issues put before them in a defamation case. If a jury trial is waived, the judge performs both functions.

The major issues to be decided in defamation cases include:

Determination of Meaning and Defamatory Character of Communication

It is the function of the judge to determine whether a communication is capable of bearing a particular meaning and whether that meaning is defamatory.

It is the function of the jury to determine whether a communication, capable of a defamatory meaning, was understood as such by the recipient.

See §614 of the Restatement Second of Torts set forth in the Appendix.

Determination of Slander Actionable Per Se

It is the function of the judge to determine whether a crime, a disease, or a type of sexual misconduct imputed by spoken language is of such a character as to make the slander actionable per se.

It is the function of the jury to determine, subject to the control of the court whenever the issue arises, whether the spoken language imputes to another conduct, characteristics or a condition incompatible with the proper conduct of the plaintiff's business, trade, profession or office.

See §615 of the Restatement Second of Torts set forth in the Appendix.

Determination of Damages

It is the function of the judge to determine what items of harm suffered by the plaintiff as the result of the publication of the defamatory matter may be considered by the jury in assessing damages.

It is the function of the jury to determine the amount of damages to be awarded for those items.

See §616 of the Restatement Second of Torts set forth in the Appendix.

Determination of Publication, Truth and Defendant's Fault

It is the function of the jury, subject to the control of the court whenever the issue arises, to determine whether the defamatory matter was published *of and concerning* the plaintiff; whether the matter was true or false; and whether the defendant had the requisite fault in regard to the truth or falsity of the matter and its defamatory character.

See §617 of the Restatement Second of Torts set forth in the Appendix.

Determination of Privileges

It is the function of the judge to determine whether the occasion upon which the defendant published the defamatory matter gives rise to a privilege.

It is the function of the jury, subject to the control of the court whenever the issues arises, to determine whether the defendant abused a conditional privilege.

See §619 of the Restatement Second of Torts set forth in the Appendix.

APPENDICIES

APPENDIX 1:

STATE STATUTES OF LIMITATIONS FOR DEFAMATION CLAIMS

STATE	LIMITATIONS PERIOD
Alabama	2 YEARS
Alaska	2 YEARS
Arizona	1 YEAR
Arkansas	1 YEAR FOR SLANDER / 3 YEARS FOR LIBEL
California	1 YEAR
Colorado	1 YEAR
Connecticut	2 YEARS
Delaware	2 YEARS
District of Columbia	1 YEAR
Florida	2 YEARS
Georgia	1 YEAR
Hawaii	2 YEARS
Idaho	2 YEARS
Illinois	1 YEAR
Indiana	2 YEARS
Iowa	2 YEARS
Kansas	1 YEAR
Kentucky	1 YEAR
Louisiana	1 YEAR
Maine	2 YEARS
Maryland	1 YEAR
Massachusetts	3 YEARS
Michigan	1 YEAR
Minnesota	2 YEARS
Mississippi	1 YEAR
Missouri	2 YEARS
Montana	2 YEARS
Nebraska	1 YEAR
Nevada	2 YEARS
New Hampshire	3 YEARS
New Jersey	1 YEAR
New Mexico	3 YEARS
New York	1 YEAR
North Carolina	1 YEAR
North Dakota	2 YEARS
Ohio	1 YEAR
Oklahoma	1 YEAR
Oregon	1 YEAR
Pennsylvania	1 YEAR

Rhode Island
1 YEAR FOR
SLANDER
3 YEARS FOR LIBEL

South Carolina
2 YEARS

South Dakota
2 YEARS

Tennessee
6 MONTHS FOR
SLANDER
1 YEAR FOR LIBEL

Texas
1 YEAR

Utah
1 YEAR

Vermont
3 YEARS

Virginia
2 YEARS

Washington
2 YEARS

West Virginia
1 YEAR

Wisconsin
2 YEARS

Wyoming
1 YEAR

APPENDIX 2:

SAMPLE COMPLAINT FOR LIBEL

[NAME OF COURT]

[CAPTION OF CASE]

COMPLAINT

INDEX NO:

The plaintiff, complaining of the defendant by his attorney, [name of attorney], herein states the following:

1. At all times hereinafter mentioned, the plaintiff was and still is a resident of the Town of _____, County of _____, State of _____.

2. At all times hereinafter mentioned, the plaintiff was and still is engaged in the accounting business in _____, and elsewhere, with their principal place of business in the Town of _____, County of _____, State of _____.

3. Upon information and belief, at all times hereinafter mentioned, the defendant, _____ Corporation, was and still is a foreign corporation duly organized and existing under and by virtue of the laws of the State of _____, authorized and doing business in the State of New York, with its principal place of business in the Town of _____, County of _____, State of _____.

4. Upon information and belief, at all times hereinafter mentioned, the defendant, _____ Corporation, owned and published a certain newspaper known as "_____."

5. Upon information and belief, at all times hereinafter mentioned, the newspaper was published on a daily basis, and enjoyed a large circulation to the public of the Town of _____,

County of _____, State of _____, and elsewhere in the United States.

6. Upon information and belief, at all times hereinafter mentioned, all or some of the individual defendants were and still are residents of the State of _____.

7. Upon information and belief, at all times hereinafter mentioned, the defendant _____, was the Editor and Publisher of the newspaper.

8. Upon information and belief, at all times hereinafter mentioned, the defendant _____, was a reporter for the newspaper.

9. Upon information and belief, at all times hereinafter mentioned, the defendant _____, was a writer for the newspaper.

10. On the ____ day of _____, 19___, the defendant _____ Corporation published and circulated in the newspaper a false, defamatory, malicious, and libelous article of and concerning the plaintiff, a copy of which is attached hereto as Plaintiff's Exhibit A.

11. On the ____ day of _____, 19___, the individual defendants participated in the preparation and publication of the false, defamatory, malicious, and libelous article of and concerning the plaintiff, which article contains the following matter, to wit: [Set forth details of defamatory statements contained in the article].

12. Upon information and belief, at the time of the aforesaid publications, the defendants were actuated by actual malice in that the defendants knew that the article and matters contained therein concerning the plaintiff so published, was false and untrue, or was published with reckless and wanton disregard of whether they were false and untrue.

13. As a result of the publication and the acts of the defendants in connection therewith, the plaintiff has been held up to public

SAMPLE COMPLAINT FOR LIBEL

contempt, ridicule, disgrace and prejudice; has suffered great mental pain and anguish; and has been irreparably injured in his good name, business reputation, and social standing, and has lost the esteem and respect of his friends, acquaintances, business associates, and of the public generally.

14. By reason of the foregoing, plaintiff has been greatly injured and damaged, and, in addition, is entitled to punitive damages against the defendants, all in the sum of _____ ($_____) Dollars.

WHEREFORE, plaintiff demands judgment against the defendant, and each of them, including punitive damages, in the sum of _____ ($_____) Dollars, plus interest, the costs and disbursements of this action, and such other and further relief as the Court deems just and proper.

[Name of Attorney]

Attorney for Plaintiff

[Attorney's Address]

[Attorney's Telephone Number]

---

[1] Source: Adapted from West's McKinney's Forms, Civil Practice Law and Rules, Volume 1A, West Publishing Company, 1992.

APPENDIX 3:

SAMPLE COMPLAINT FOR SLANDER

[NAME OF COURT]

[CAPTION OF CASE]

COMPLAINT

INDEX NO:

The plaintiff, complaining of the defendant by his attorney, [name of attorney], herein states the following:

1. The plaintiff was and still is engaged as a carpenter in the Town of _____, County of_____, State of _____; that he has conducted that business and trade in that town and in and about _____ and adjoining counties for many years prior to the utterance of the false and defamatory words hereinafter set forth and has always borne a good reputation, for honesty and uprightness in his dealings with the public and a good reputation and credit as a businessman and otherwise.

2. Upon information and belief, at all times hereinafter mentioned, the defendant _____, was and still is a resident of the State of _____.

3. That during the past several years the plaintiff has done carpentry work and furnished materials to the defendant, and to others.

4. That on or about the___day of _____, 19_____, at _____ o'clock, the defendant, in connection with the carpentry work performed and the materials furnished to the defendant and others, and in the presence of several persons, maliciously spoke of and concerning the plaintiff, and his business and trade as

a carpenter, the following false and defamatory words: [Quote defamatory statement made].

5. That the words so spoken were false and defamatory, were known to the defendant to be false and defamatory, and were spoken willfully and maliciously with the intent to damage the plaintiff's good name and reputation as a carpenter.

6. That by reason of the words so spoken by the defendant, plaintiff has been injured in his good name and reputation as a carpenter and has suffered great pain and mental anguish and has been held up to ridicule and contempt by his friends, acquaintances, and the public, all to his damage in the sum of _____ ($_____) Dollars.

WHEREFORE, plaintiff demands judgment against the defendant in the sum of _____ ($_____) Dollars, plus interest, the costs and disbursements of this action, and such other and further relief as the Court deems just and proper.

[Name of Attorney]

Attorney for Plaintiff

[Attorney's Address]

[Attorney's Telephone Number]

1

---

[1] Source: Adapted from West's McKinney's Forms, Civil Practice Law and Rules, Volume 1A, West Publishing Company, 1992.

APPENDIX 4:

FIRST AMENDMENT TO THE UNITED STATES CONSTITUTION

Congress shall make no law respecting an establishment of religion, or prohibiting the free exercise thereof; *or abridging the freedom of speech, or of the press*, or the right of the people peaceably to assemble, and to petition the Government for a redress of grievances.

APPENDIX 5:

FOURTEENTH AMENDMENT TO THE UNITED STATES CONSTITUTION

Section 1. All persons born or naturalized in the United States and subject to the jurisdiction thereof, are citizens of the United States and of the State wherein they reside. No State shall make or enforce any law which shall abridge the privileges or immunities of citizens of the United States; nor shall any State deprive any person of life, liberty, or property, without due process of law; nor deny to any person within its jurisdiction the equal protection of the laws.

APPENDIX 6:

THE SPEECH OR DEBATE CLAUSE OF THE UNITED STATES CONSTITUTION

Article I, Section 6. The Senators and Representatives shall receive a compensation for their services, to be ascertained by law, and paid out of the Treasury of the United States. They shall in all cases, except treason, felony and breach of the peace, be privileged from arrest during their attendance at the session of their respective Houses, and in going to and returning from the same; and for any *Speech or Debate* in either House, they shall not be questioned in any other place.

APPENDIX 7:

APPLICABLE SECTIONS OF THE RESTATEMENT SECOND OF THE LAW OF TORTS

SECTION 558: ELEMENTS STATED

To create liability for defamation there must be:

(a) a false and defamatory statement concerning another;

(b) an unprivileged publication to a third party;

(c) fault amounting at least to negligence on the part of the publisher; and

(d) either actionability of the statement irrespective of special harm or the existence of special harm caused by the publication.

SECTION 559: DEFAMATORY COMMUNICATION DEFINED

A communication is defamatory if it tends so to harm the reputation of another as to lower him in the estimation of the community or to deter third persons from associating or dealing with him.

SECTION 560: DEFAMATION OF DECEASED PERSONS

One who publishes defamatory matter concerning a deceased person is not liable either to the estate of the person or to his descendants or relatives.

SECTION 568: LIBEL AND SLANDER DISTINGUISHED

(1) Libel consists of the publication of defamatory matter by written or printed words, by its embodiment in physical form or by

any other form of communication that has the potentially harmful qualities characteristic of written or printed words.

(2) Slander consists of the publication of defamatory matter by spoken words, transitory gestures or by any form of communication other than those stated in Subsection (1).

(3) The area of dissemination, the deliberate and premeditated character of its publication and the persistence of the defamation are factors to be considered in determining whether a publication is a libel rather than a slander.

SECTION 569: LIABILITY WITHOUT PROOF OF SPECIAL HARM - LIBEL

One who falsely publishes matter defamatory of another in such a manner as to make the publication a libel is subject to liability to the other although no special harm results from the publication.

SECTION 570: LIABILITY WITHOUT PROOF OF SPECIAL HARM - SLANDER

One who publishes matter defamatory to another in such a manner as to make the publication a slander is subject to liability to the other although no special harm results if the publication imputes to the other:

(a) a criminal offense, as stated in §571, or

(b) a loathsome disease, as stated in §572, or

(c) matter incompatible with his business, trade, profession, or office, as stated in §573, or

(d) serious sexual misconduct, as stated in §574.

SECTION 571: SLANDEROUS IMPUTATIONS OF CRIMINAL CONDUCT

One who publishes a slander that imputes to another conduct constituting a criminal offense is subject to liability to the other without proof of special harm if the offense imputed is of a type which, if committed in the place of publication, would be:

(a) punishable by imprisonment in a state or federal institution, or

(b) regarded by public opinion as involving moral turpitude.

SECTION 572: SLANDEROUS IMPUTATIONS OF LOATHSOME DISEASE

One who publishes a slander that imputes to another an existing venereal disease or other loathsome and communicable disease is subject to liability without proof of special harm.

SECTION 573: SLANDEROUS IMPUTATIONS AFFECTING BUSINESS, TRADE, PROFESSION OR OFFICE

One who publishes a slander that ascribes to another conduct, characteristics or a condition that would adversely affect his fitness for the proper conduct of his lawful business, trade or profession, or of his public or private office, whether honorary or for profit, is subject to liability without proof of special harm.

SECTION 574: SLANDEROUS IMPUTATIONS OF SEXUAL MISCONDUCT

One who publishes a slander that imputes serious sexual misconduct to another is subject to liability to the other without proof of special harm.

SECTION 575: SLANDER CREATING LIABILITY BECAUSE OF SPECIAL HARM

One who publishes a slander that, although not actionable per se, is the legal cause of special harm to the person defamed, is subject to liability to him.

SECTION 576: HARM CAUSED BY REPETITION

The publication of a libel or slander is a legal cause of any special harm resulting from its repetition by a third person if, but only if:

(a) the third person was privileged to repeat it, or

(b) the repetition was authorized or intended by the original defamer, or

(c) the repetition was reasonably to be expected.

SECTION 577A: SINGLE AND MULTIPLE PUBLICATIONS

(1) Except as stated in Subsections (2) and (3), each of several communications to a third person by the same defamer is a separate publication.

(2) A single communication heard at the same time by two or more third persons is a single publication.

(3) Any one edition of a book or newspaper, or any one radio or television broadcast, exhibition of a motion picture or similar aggregate communication is a single publication.

(4) As to any single publication:

(a) only one action for damages can be maintained;

(b) all damages suffered in all jurisdictions can be recovered in the one action; and

(c) a judgment for or against the plaintiff upon the merits of any action for damages bars any other action for damages between the same parties in all jurisdictions.

SECTION 578: LIABILITY OF REPUBLISHER

Except as to those who only deliver or transmit defamation published by a third person, one who repeats or otherwise republishes defamatory matter is subject to liability as if he had originally published it.

SECTION 580A: DEFAMATION OF PUBLIC OFFICIAL OR PUBLIC FIGURE

One who publishes a false and defamatory communication concerning a public official or public figure in regard to his conduct, fitness or role in that capacity is subject to liability, if, but only if, he:

(a) knows that the statement is false and that it defames the other person, or

(b) acts in reckless disregard of these matters.

SECTION 580B: DEFAMATION OF PRIVATE PERSON

One who publishes a false and defamatory communication concerning a private person, or concerning a public official or public figure in relation to a purely private matter not affecting his conduct, fitness or role in his public capacity, is subject to liability, if, but only if, he:

(a) knows that the statement is false and that it defames the other,

(b) acts in reckless disregard of these matters, or

(c) acts negligently in failing to ascertain them.

SECTION 581A: TRUE STATEMENTS

One who publishes a defamatory statement of fact is not subject to liability for defamation if the statement is true.

TITLE A: CONSENT

SECTION 583: GENERAL PRINCIPLE

Except as stated in §584, the consent of another to the publication of defamatory matter concerning him is a complete defense to his action for defamation.

TITLE B: ABSOLUTE PRIVILEGE IRRESPECTIVE OF CONSENT

SECTION 585: JUDICIAL OFFICERS

A judge or other officer performing a judicial function is absolutely privileged to publish defamatory matter in the performance of the function if the publication has some relation to the matter before him.

TITLE B: ABSOLUTE PRIVILEGE IRRESPECTIVE OF CONSENT

SECTION 586: ATTORNEYS AT LAW

An attorney at law is absolutely privileged to publish defamatory matter concerning another in communications preliminary to a proposed judicial proceeding, or in the institution of, or during the course and as a part of, a judicial proceeding in which he participates as counsel, if it has some relation to the proceeding.

APPLICABLE SECTIONS

TITLE B: ABSOLUTE PRIVILEGE IRRESPECTIVE OF CONSENT

SECTION 587: PARTIES TO JUDICIAL PROCEEDINGS

A party to a private litigation or a private prosecutor or defendant in a criminal prosecution is absolutely privileged to publish defamatory matter concerning another in communications preliminary to a proposed judicial proceeding, or in the institution of or during the course and as a part of, a judicial proceeding in which he participates, if the matter has some relation to the proceeding.

TITLE B: ABSOLUTE PRIVILEGE IRRESPECTIVE OF CONSENT

SECTION 588: WITNESSES IN JUDICIAL PROCEEDINGS

A witness is absolutely privileged to publish defamatory matter concerning another in communications preliminary to a proposed judicial proceeding or as a part of a judicial proceeding in which he is testifying, if it has some relation to the proceeding.

TITLE B: ABSOLUTE PRIVILEGE IRRESPECTIVE OF CONSENT

SECTION 589: JURORS

A member of a grand or petit jury is absolutely privileged to publish defamatory matter concerning another in the performance of his function as a juror, if the defamatory matter has some relation to the proceedings in which he is acting as juror.

TITLE B: ABSOLUTE PRIVILEGE IRRESPECTIVE OF CONSENT

SECTION 590: LEGISLATORS

A member of the Congress of the United States or of a State or local legislative body is absolutely privileged to publish defamatory matter concerning another in the performance of his legislative functions.

TITLE B: ABSOLUTE PRIVILEGE IRRESPECTIVE OF CONSENT

SECTION 590A: WITNESSES IN LEGISLATIVE PROCEEDINGS

A witness is absolutely privileged to publish defamatory matter as part of a legislative proceeding in which he is testifying or in communications preliminary to the proceeding, if the matter has some relation to the proceeding.

TITLE B: ABSOLUTE PRIVILEGE IRRESPECTIVE OF CONSENT

SECTION 591: EXECUTIVE AND ADMINISTRATIVE OFFICERS

An absolute privilege to publish defamatory matter concerning another in communications made in the performance of his official duties exists for:

(a) any executive or administrative officer of the United States; or

(b) a governor or other superior executive officer of a state.

APPLICABLE SECTIONS

TITLE B: ABSOLUTE PRIVILEGE IRRESPECTIVE OF CONSENT

SECTION 592: HUSBAND AND WIFE

A husband or a wife is absolutely privileged to publish to the other spouse defamatory matter concerning a third person.

TITLE B: ABSOLUTE PRIVILEGE IRRESPECTIVE OF CONSENT

SECTION 592A: PUBLICATION REQUIRED BY LAW

One who is required by law to publish defamatory matter is absolutely privileged to publish it.

SECTION 594: PROTECTION OF THE PUBLISHER'S INTEREST

An occasion makes a publication conditionally privileged if the circumstances induce a correct or reasonable belief that:

(a) there is information that affects a sufficiently important interest of the publisher; and

(b) the recipient's knowledge of the defamatory matter will be of service in the lawful protection of the interest.

SECTION 595: PROTECTION OF INTEREST OF RECIPIENT OR A THIRD PERSON

(1) An occasion makes a publication conditionally privileged if the circumstances induce a correct or reasonable belief that:

(a) there is information that affects a sufficiently important interest of the recipient or a third person, and

(b) the recipient is one to whom the publisher is under a legal duty to publish the defamatory matter or is a person to whom its publication is otherwise within the generally accepted standards of decent conduct.

(2) In determining whether a publication is within generally accepted standards of decent conduct it is an important factor that:

(a) the publication is made in response to a request rather than volunteered by the publisher, or

(b) a family or other relationship exists between the parties.

SECTION 596: COMMON INTEREST

An occasion makes a publication conditionally privileged if the circumstances lead any one of several persons having a common interest in a particular subject matter correctly or reasonably to believe that there is information that another sharing the common interest is entitled to know.

SECTION 597: FAMILY RELATIONSHIPS

(1) An occasion makes a publication conditionally privileged if the circumstances induce a correct or reasonable belief that:

(a) there is information that affects the well-being of a member of the immediate family of the publisher, and

(b) the recipient's knowledge of the defamatory matter will be of service in the lawful protection of the well-being of the member of the family.

(2) An occasion makes a publication conditionally privileged when the circumstances induce a correct or reasonable belief that:

(a) there is information that affects the well-being of a member of the immediate family of the recipient or of a third person, and

(b) the recipient's knowledge of the defamatory matter will be of service in the lawful protection of the well-being of the member of the family, and

(c) the recipient has requested the publication of the defamatory matter or is a person to whom its publication is otherwise within generally accepted standards of decent conduct.

SECTION 598: COMMUNICATION TO ONE WHO MAY ACT IN THE PUBLIC INTEREST

An occasion makes a publication conditionally privileged if the circumstances induce a correct or reasonable belief that:

(a) there is information that affects a sufficiently important public interest, and

(b) the public interest requires the communication of the defamatory matter to a public officer or a private citizen who is authorized or privileged to take action if the defamatory matter is true.

SECTION 598A: INFERIOR STATE OFFICERS

An occasion makes a publication conditionally privileged if an inferior administrative officer of a state or any of its subdivisions who is not entitled to an absolute privilege makes a defamatory communication required or permitted in the performance of his official duties.

SECTION 600: KNOWLEDGE OF FALSITY OR RECKLESS DISREGARD AS TO TRUTH

Except as stated in §682, one who upon an occasion giving rise to a conditional privilege publishes false and defamatory matter concerning another abuses the privilege if he

(a) knows the matter to be false, or

(b) acts in reckless disregard as to its truth or falsity.

SECTION 602: PUBLICATION OF A DEFAMATORY RUMOR

One who upon an occasion giving rise to a conditional privilege publishes a defamatory rumor or suspicion concerning another does not abuse the privilege, even if he knows or believes the rumor or suspicion to be false, if:

(a) he states the defamatory matter as rumor or suspicion and not as fact, and

(b) the relation of the parties, the importance of the interests affected, and the harm likely to be done make the publication reasonable.

SECTION 603: PURPOSE OF THE PRIVILEGE

One who upon an occasion giving rise to a conditional privilege publishes defamatory matter concerning another abuses the privilege if he does not act for the purpose of protecting the interest for the protection of which the privilege is given.

SECTION 604: EXCESSIVE PUBLICATION

One who, upon an occasion giving rise to a conditional privilege for the publication of defamatory matter to a particular person or persons, knowingly publishes the matter to a person to whom its publication is not otherwise privileged, abuses the privilege unless he reasonably believes that the publication is a proper means of communicating the defamatory matter to the person to whom its publication is privileged.

SECTION 605: NECESSITY FOR PUBLICATION AND PURPOSE OF PRIVILEGE

One who upon an occasion giving rise to a conditional privilege publishes defamatory matter concerning another, abuses the privilege if he does not reasonably believe the matter to be necessary to accomplish the purpose for which the privilege is given.

SECTION 613: BURDEN OF PROOF

(1) In an action for defamation the plaintiff has the burden of proving, when the issue is properly raised:

(a) the defamatory character of the communication,

(b) its publication by the defendant,

(c) its application to the plaintiff,

(d) the recipient's understanding of its defamatory meaning,

(e) the recipient's understanding of it as intended to be applied to the plaintiff,

(f) special harm resulting to the plaintiff from its publication,

(g) the defendant's negligence, reckless disregard or knowledge regarding the truth or falsity and the defamatory character of the communication, and

(h) the abuse of a conditional privilege.

(2) In an action for defamation the defendant has the burden of proving, when the issue is properly raised, the presence of the circumstances necessary for the existence of a privilege to publish the defamatory communication.

SECTION 614: DETERMINATION OF MEANING AND DEFAMATORY CHARACTER OF COMMUNICATION

(1) The court determines:

(a) whether a communication is capable of bearing a particular meaning, and

(b) whether that meaning is defamatory.

(2) The jury determines whether a communication, capable of a defamatory meaning, was so understood by its recipient.

SECTION 615: DETERMINATION OF SLANDER ACTIONABLE PER SE

(1) The court determines whether a crime, a disease or a type of sexual misconduct imputed by spoken language is of such a character as to make the slander actionable per se.

(2) Subject to the control of the court whenever the issue arises, the jury determines whether spoken language imputes to another conduct, characteristics or a condition incompatible with the proper conduct of his business, trade, profession or office.

SECTION 616: DETERMINATION OF DAMAGES

The Court determines what items of harm suffered by the plaintiff as the result of the publication of the defamatory matter may be considered by the jury in assessing damages; the jury determines the amount of damages to be awarded for those items.

SECTION 617: PUBLICATION, TRUTH AND DEFENDANT'S FAULT

Subject to the control of the court whenever the issue arises, the jury determines whether:

(a) the defamatory matter was published of and concerning the plaintiff;

(b) the matter was true or false; and

(c) the defendant had the requisite fault in regard to the truth or falsity of the matter and its defamatory character.

SECTION 619: PRIVILEGES

(1) The court determines whether the occasion upon which the defendant published the defamatory matter gives rise to a privilege.

(2) Subject to the control of the court whenever the issue arises, the jury determines whether the defendant abused a conditional privilege.

SECTION 620: NOMINAL DAMAGES

One who is liable for a slander actionable per se or for a libel is liable for at least nominal damages.

SECTION 621: GENERAL DAMAGES

One who is liable for a defamatory communication is liable for the proved, actual harm caused to the reputation of the person defamed.

SECTION 622: SPECIAL HARM AS AFFECTING THE MEASURE OF RECOVERY

One who is liable for either a slander actionable per se or a libel is also liable for any special harm legally caused by the defamatory publication.

SECTION 622A: LEGAL CAUSATION OF SPECIAL HARM

Defamation is a legal cause of special harm to the person defamed if:

(a) it is a substantial factor in bringing about the harm, and

(b) there is no rule of law relieving the publisher from liability because of the manner in which the publication has resulted in the harm.

SECTION 623: EMOTIONAL DISTRESS AND RESULTING BODILY HARM

One who is liable to another for a libel or slander is liable also for emotional distress and bodily harm that is proved to have been caused by the defamatory publication.

GLOSSARY

GLOSSARY

Absolute Privilege - The privilege to speak or publish defamatory words without liability, and without reference to the speaker or publisher's motives, or the truth or falsity of the statement.

Actionable Per Quod - Words which are not clearly actionable but which become so when considered in connection with innuendo, colloquium and explanatory circumstances.

Actionable Per Se - Words which the law presumes must actually, proximately and necessarily damage the defendant, for which general damages are recoverable, and whose injurious character is a fact of common notoriety.

Actionable Words - In the law of libel and slander, refers to words which naturally imply damage.

Action at Law - A judicial proceeding whereby one party prosecutes another for a wrong done.

Actionable - Giving rise to a cause of action.

Actual Damages - Actual damages are those damages directly referable to the breach or tortious act, and which can be readily proven to have been sustained, and for which the injured party should be compensated as a matter of right.

Actual Malice - In defamation law, the standard of malice required to be liable for defamatory statements made concerning public officials or public figures, which standard requires knowledge of the falsity of the statement, or reckless disregard to its truth or falsity.

Ad Damnum Clause - The clause in a complaint which sets forth the amount of damages demanded.

Adjudication - The determination of a controversy and pronouncement of judgment.

Admissible Evidence - Evidence which may be received by a trial court to assist the trier of fact, either the judge or jury, in deciding a dispute.

Adversary - Opponent or litigant in a legal controversy or litigation.

Adversary Proceeding - A proceeding involving a real controversy contested by two opposing parties.

Affirmative Defense - In a pleading, a matter constituting a defense.

Agent - One who represents another known as the principal.

Answer - In a civil proceeding, the principal pleading on the part of the defendant in response to the plaintiff's complaint.

Apparent Agency - Apparent agency exists when one person, whether or not authorized, reasonably appears to a third person to be authorized to act as agent for such other.

Appeal - Resort to a higher court for the purpose of obtaining a review of a lower court decision.

Appearance - To come into court, personally or through an attorney, after being summoned.

Appellate Court - A court having jurisdiction to review the law as applied to a prior determination of the same case.

Argument - A discourse set forth for the purpose of establishing one's position in a controversy.

Bench - The court and the judges composing the court collectively.

Burden of Proof - The duty of a party to substantiate an allegation or issue to convince the trier of fact as to the truth of their claim.

Caption - The heading of a legal document which contains the name of the court, the index number assigned to the matter, and the names of the parties.

GLOSSARY

Cause of Action - The factual basis for bringing a lawsuit.

Certiorari - A common law writ whereby a higher court requests a review of a lower court's records to determine whether any irregularities occurred in a particular proceeding.

Chief Justice - The presiding member of certain courts which have more than one judge, e.g., the United States Supreme Court.

Circuit - A judicial division of a state or the United States.

Circuit Court - One of several courts in a given jurisdiction.

Circumstantial Evidence - Indirect evidence by which a principal fact may be inferred.

Citation - A reference to a source of legal authority, such as a case or statute.

Civil Action - An action maintained to protect a private, civil right as opposed to a criminal action.

Civil Court - The court designed to resolve disputes arising under the common law and civil statutes.

Civil Law - Law which applies to noncriminal actions.

Civil Penalty - A fine imposed as punishment for a certain activity.

Claimant - The party who brings the arbitration petition, also known as the plaintiff.

Common Law - Common law is the system of jurisprudence which originated in England and was later applied in the United States.

Compensatory Damages - Compensatory damages are those damages directly referable to a breach or tortious act, and which can be readily proven to have been sustained, and for which the injured party should be compensated as a matter of right.

Complaint - In a civil proceeding, the first pleading of the plaintiff setting out the facts on which the claim for relief is based.

Conclusion of Fact - A conclusion reached by natural inference and based solely on the facts presented.

Conclusion of Law - A conclusion reached through the application of rules of law.

Conclusive Evidence - Evidence which is incontrovertible.

Condition - A condition is a future and uncertain event upon the happening of which some obligation is contingent.

Conditional Privilege - The privilege to speak or publish defamatory words without liability provided the speaker or publisher is without malice and unaware of the falsity of the statement.

Consequential Damages - Consequential damages are those damages which are caused by an injury, but which are not a necessary result of the injury, and must be specially pleaded and proven in order to be awarded.

Constitution - The fundamental principles of law which frame a governmental system.

Constitutional Right - Refers to the individual liberties granted by the constitution of a state or the federal government.

Criminal Libel - The malicious publication of durable defamation which is generally a misdemeanor at common law and under modern statutes and requires the elements of defamation, durability, publication, and malice.

Cross-Examination - The questioning of a witness by someone other than the one who called the witness to the stand concerning matters about which the witness testified during direct examination.

Damages - In general, damages refers to monetary compensation which the law awards to one who has been injured by the actions of

GLOSSARY

another, such as in the case of tortious conduct or breach of contractual obligations.

Decedent - A deceased person.

Defamation - The publication of a false and injurious statement about the reputation of another. Includes both libel and slander.

Defamation Per Quod - Words which require an allegation of facts, aside from the words contained in the publication, by way of innuendo, to show how the words libel the plaintiff.

Defamation Per Se - Words which by themselves, without reference to extrinsic proof, injure the reputation of the person to whom they are applied.

Defamatory - Injurious to reputation.

Defamatory Communication - A communication which tends to so harm the reputation of another as to lower him in the estimation of the community or to deter third persons from associating or dealing with him.

Defamatory Libel - Written, permanent form of defamation as contrasted with slander which is oral defamation.

Defendant - In a civil proceeding, the party responding to the complaint.

Defense - Opposition to the truth or validity of the plaintiff's claims.

Ecclesiastical Law - The body of jurisprudence administered by the ecclesiastical courts of England derived from the canon and civil law.

Fact Finding - A process by which parties present their evidence and make their arguments to a neutral person, who issues a non-binding report based on the findings, which usually contains a recommendation for settlement.

Federal Courts - The courts of the United States.

Finding - Decisions made by the court on issues of fact or law.

First Amendment - Amendment to the U.S. Constitution guaranteeing basic freedoms of speech, religion, press, and assembly and the right to petition the government for redress of grievances.

Fourteenth Amendment - Amendment to the U.S. Constitution which forbids the making or enforcement by any state of any law abridging the privileges and immunities of citizens of the United States, and secures all persons against any state action which results in either deprivation of life, liberty, or property without due process of law, or, in denial of the equal protection of the laws.

General Damages - General damages are those damages directly referable to the breach or tortious act and which can be readily proven to have been sustained, and for which the injured party should be compensated as a matter of right.

Group Libel - The holding up of a group to ridicule, scorn or contempt to a respectable and considerable part of the community.

Hearing - A proceeding during which evidence is taken for the purpose of determining the facts of a dispute and reaching a decision.

Impaneling - Selecting and swearing in a panel of jurors for duty.

Impeach - A showing by means of evidence that the testimony of a witness was unworthy of belief. Also refers to the process of charging a public official with a wrong while still holding office.

Implied Consent - Consent which is manifested by signs, actions or facts, or by inaction or silence, which raises a presumption that consent has been given.

Injunction - A judicial remedy either requiring a party to perform an act, or restricting a party from continuing a particular act.

GLOSSARY

Injury - Any damage done to another's person, rights, reputation or property.

Innuendo - In a defamation action, a statement of construction put forth by the plaintiff to show that words which appear innocent on their own are actually libelous.

Instruction - Directions concerning the applicable law of a case, which are given to the jury by the judge prior to their deliberation.

Insufficient Evidence - The judicial decision that the evidence submitted to prove a case does not meet the degree necessary to go forward with the action.

Intentional Tort - A tort or wrong perpetrated by one who intends to do that which the law has declared wrong, as contrasted with negligence in which the tortfeasor fails to exercise that degree of care in doing what is otherwise permissible.

Issue Preclusion - The doctrine which states that an issue which has already been decided cannot be relitigated.

Judge - The individual who presides over a court, and whose function it is to determine controversies.

Judgment - A judgment is a final determination by a court of law concerning the rights of the parties to a lawsuit.

Judicial Notice - The doctrine whereby the court takes note of certain facts which are indisputable thereby relieving one party of the burden of proving the fact.

Jurisdiction - The power to hear and determine a case.

Jury - A group of individuals summoned to decide the facts in issue in a lawsuit.

Jury Trial - A trial during which the evidence is presented to a jury so that they can determine the issues of fact, and render a verdict based upon the law as it applies to their findings of fact.

Liability - Liability refers to one's obligation to do or refrain from doing something, such as the payment of a debt.

Libel - The false and unprivileged publication in writing of defamatory material.

Libelous - Defamatory.

Libelous Per Quod - Publications which are not obviously defamatory but which become so when considered in connection with innuendo, colloquium and explanatory circumstances.

Libelous Per Se - A publication wherein the words are of such a character than an action may be brought upon them without the necessity of showing any special damage, the imputation being such that the law will presume one must have suffered damage.

Malice - In a defamation action, simple malice refers to an evil intent or motive arising from spite or ill will.

Misdemeanor - Criminal offenses which are less serious than felonies and carry lesser penalties.

Mitigation of Damages - The requirement that a person damaged due to another's acts, such as a breach of contract, must act reasonably to avoid or limit their losses, or risk denial of recovery for damages which could have been avoided.

Negligence - The failure to exercise the degree of care which a reasonable person would exercise given the same circumstances.

Negligence Per Se - Conduct, whether of action or omission, which may be declared and treated as negligence without any argument or proof as to the particular surrounding circumstances, because it is contrary to the law.

Nominal Damages - A trivial sum of money which is awarded as recognition that a legal injury was sustained, although slight.

Obscene Libel - The type of defamation which holds a person up to ridicule, scorn or contempt to a considerable and respectable

GLOSSARY

class in the community, by printed words or configurations of a lewd and lascivious nature.

Obscene Material - Material which lacks serious literary, artistic, political or scientific value and, taken as a whole, appeals to the prurient interest and, as such, is not protected by the free speech guarantee of the First Amendment.

Opinion - The reasoning behind a court's decision.

Pecuniary - A term relating to monetary matters.

Plaintiff - In a civil proceeding, the one who initially brings the lawsuit.

Pleadings - Refers to plaintiff's complaint which sets forth the facts of the cause of action, and defendant's answer which sets forth the responses and defenses to the allegations contained in the complaint.

Prima Facie Case - A case which is sufficient on its face, being supported by at least the requisite minimum of evidence, and being free from palpable defects.

Privilege - In defamation law, an exemption from liability for the speaking or publishing of defamatory words concerning another, based on the fact that the statement was made in the performance of a political, judicial, social or personal duty.

Publication - In defamation law, the act of making defamatory matter known publicly, or disseminating it, or communicating it to one or more persons.

Punitive Damages - Compensation in excess of compensatory damages which serves as a form of punishment to the wrongdoer who has exhibited malicious and willful misconduct.

Question of Fact - The fact in dispute which is the province of the trier of fact, i.e. the judge or jury, to decide.

Question of Law - The question of law which is the province of the judge to decide.

Reporter's Privilege - In defamation law, the rule that the publisher is conditionally protected in actions of defamation if the publication constitutes fair comment on the subject matter of public officers and employees in matters of public concern.

Respondent - The responding party, also known as the defendant.

Restatement of the Law - A series of volumes authored by the American Law Institute that tell what the law in a general area is, how it is changing, and what direction the authors think this change should take.

Retraction - In defamation law, a formal recanting of defamatory material which, although not a defense, may serve to mitigate damages.

Seditious Libel - A communication written with the intent to incite the people to change the government otherwise than by lawful means, or to advocate the overthrow of the government by force or violence.

Settlement - An agreement by the parties to a dispute on a resolution of the claims, usually requiring some mutual action, such as payment of money in consideration of a release of claims.

Single Publication Rule - In defamation law, where an issue of a newspaper or magazine, or an edition of a book, contains a libelous statement, rule that plaintiff has a single cause of action, and the number of copies distributed while relevant for damages, is not a basis for a new cause of action.

Slander - The speaking of false and malicious words concerning another whereby injury results to his reputation.

Slanderer - One who commits slander.

GLOSSARY

Slander of title - A false and malicious statement, oral or written, made in disparagement of a person's title to real or personal property, or of some other right, thus causing him special damage.

Slanderous Per Se - Words which are deemed slanderous without proof of special damages.

Sovereign Immunity - A doctrine which prohibits lawsuits against the government without its consent.

Speech of Debate Clause - Section of the U.S. Constitution which grants congressmen immunity for any speech or debate in either House.

Statute of Limitations - Any law which fixes the time within which parties must take judicial action to enforce rights or thereafter be barred from enforcing them.

Survival Statute - A statute that preserves for a decedent's estate a cause of action for infliction of pain and suffering and related damages suffered up to the moment of death.

Tort - A private or civil wrong or injury, other than breach of contract, for which the court will provide a remedy in the form of an action for damages.

Tort Claims Act - A statute passed by Congress which waives the government's sovereign immunity from tort liability.

Tortfeasor - A wrongdoer.

Tortious Conduct - Wrongful conduct, whether of act or omission, of such a character as to subject the actor to liability under the law of torts.

Unconstitutional - Refers to a statute which conflicts with the United States Constitution rendering it void.

United States Constitution - The charter of government agreed upon by the people of the United States as the absolute rule of action and decision for all branches of government in respect to all points covered by it, which must control until changed by the authority which established it, e.g. by amendment.

United States Supreme Court - The highest court in the United States encompassing the Chief Justice and eight Associate Justices.

Venue - The proper place for trial of a lawsuit.

Verdict - The definitive answer given by the jury to the court concerning the matters of fact committed to the jury for their deliberation and determination.

Wanton - Extremely negligent or reckless.

BIBLIOGRAPHY

Black's Law Dictionary, Fifth Edition. St. Paul, MN: West Publishing Company, 1979.

Elder, David A.*Defamation: A Lawyer's Guide.* New York, NY: Clark Boardman Callaghan, 1993.

Gifis, Steven H.*Barron's Law Dictionary, Second Ed..* Woodbury, NY: Barron's Educational Series, Inc., 1984.

Halpern, Sheldon W.*The Law of Defamation, Privacy, Publicity, and Moral Right.* Cincinnati, OH: Anderson Publishing Co., 1993.

Kane, Peter E.*Errors, Lies and Libel.* Edwardsville, IL: Southern Illinois University Press, 1992.

Kupferman, Hon. Theodore R..*Defamation: Libel and Slander.* Westport, CT: Meckler Corp., 1990.

Smolla, Rodney A.*Law of Defamation.* New York, NY: Clark Boardman Callaghan, 1991.